PRAISE
I'VE TITLED T
WITH YOUR

Anna Allen's romantic poetry compilation, *I've Titled This Poem With Your Name*, is a series of admissions more personal to the listener than diary entries or love letters left to the dial tone. Reminiscent of a modernized Sappho in 2020 American cities, Ms. Allen has crafted a voice relatable to those of us uncertain in ourselves but quite certain in our yearning. Laced with self-deprecating humor and nostalgia, her speaker grapples with identity, religion, and sexuality as a different form of worship. Fans of Ms. Allen's slam poetry performances will remain equally enthralled by her melody on paper, hearing the sensual beats and animated expressions as they follow her lead. Imbued in her pieces are mystical elements, tales of girlhood and loverhood, and the ephemeral ghosts of bad family dynamics. Alongside her first-person narrative, we experience the familiar shades of grief: reminders of "small deaths" on Earth while still breathing. Steadily returning to the bargaining phase, Ms. Allen's speaker offers both its subjects and readers increasingly vivid sacrifices just to stay connected. From the first date to the final plea, we learn moving forward sometimes means accepting love as a fist. But giving up? Not an option. Anna Allen and her poetry redefine resilience.

MADISON RUSSELL

At once self-effacing and yet simultaneously aware of her own power, the victim of both childhood trauma and the abuse from an intimate partner in her adulthood, Anna Allen unveils the dichotomies of being the "strong Black woman" and the sufferer of both physical and emotional torment from those whom she trusted most. *I've Titled This Poem With Your Name* is a love letter written by the poet, for the poet. This collection is both heartbreaking and hopeful, despairing and cathartic, and wholly transformative.

MACKENZIE EWING

I've Titled This Poem With Your Name

Anna Allen

I've Titled This Poem With Your Name

Anna Allen

**NOMADIC
PRESS**

NOMADIC PRESS

OAKLAND

111 FAIRMOUNT AVENUE
OAKLAND, CA 94611

BROOKLYN

475 KENT AVENUE #302
BROOKLYN, NY 11249

WWW.NOMADICPRESS.ORG

MASTHEAD

FOUNDING AND MANAGING EDITOR
J. K. FOWLER

ASSOCIATE EDITOR
MICHAELA MULLIN

EDITOR
NINA SACCO

MISSION STATEMENT

Nomadic Press is a 501 (C)(3) not-for-profit organization that supports the works of emerging and established writers and artists. Through publications (including translations) and performances, Nomadic Press aims to build community among artists and across disciplines.

SUBMISSIONS

Nomadic Press wholeheartedly accepts unsolicited book manuscripts. To submit your work, please visit www.nomadicpress.org/submissions

DISTRIBUTION

Orders by trade bookstores and wholesalers:
Small Press Distribution,
1341 Seventh Street
Berkeley, CA 94701
spd@spdbooks.org
(510) 524-1668 / (800) 869-7553

I've Titled This Poem With Your Name

© 2021 by Anna Allen

This book was made possible by a loving community of chosen family and friends, old and new.

For author questions or to book a reading at your bookstore, university/school, or alternative establishment, please send an email to info@nomadicpress.org.

Cover artwork and author portrait by Arthur Johnstone

Published by Nomadic Press, 111 Fairmount Avenue, Oakland, CA 94611

First printing, 2021

Printed in the United States of America

LIBRARY OF CONGRESS CATALOGING-IN-PUBLICATION DATA

Anna Allen 1990 –
Title: *I've Titled This Poem With Your Name*
P. CM.
Summary: *I've Titled This Poem With Your Name* is a collection of love notes and lovely funerals. It explores queer love and all of its politics, joy, and grief. It is a real and honest peek into queer struggles and happiness.

[1. POETRY. 2. LOVE. 3. LGBTQIA+. 4. AMERICAN GENERAL.] I. III. TITLE.

LIBRARY OF CONGRESS CONTROL NUMBER: 2021932311

ISBN: 978-1-7363963-3-9

CONTENTS

INTRODUCTION

CLASSROOM GUIDE

INTRODUCTION

I am about showcasing queer love in all of my work. This book is about that same queer love. I want to showcase the good in these poems while honestly recognizing the bad. The destruction, the offensive, the obsession, the end, and beginning again.

As a queer Black woman, I am exposed to a wide range of hate. I want to make it clear that nothing in this book is ever about hate. Even in the saddest poem here, even some of these relationships that brought to my kneecaps, I am so appreciative for all of these experiences.

TALES

I am naked in her bed
She is reading me tales
I am Dorothy
She is my Tinman
I'd crawl
hands & knees
on golden bricks
to get a heart
for that bitch

REVERSE MIDAS TOUCH

Everything is Gilded until me.
I turn golden heroes mortal.
I animate first place trophies,
the infallible suddenly furtive.

I tried wool gloves over my hands,
the fabric catching pieces of my parched skin.
But I grew lonely,
embittered,
sick of being the only best here.

I began to touch again,
watching their blank, marble eyes
fill with the watery weight of
what's to come.

THE UN-DO LIST:
THINGS I WANT TO STOP DOING

I want to stop
eating Snickers bars for breakfast

I want to stop
hitting that snooze button
every morning
12 times

I want to stop
doing that thing to my dog
where I pretend
to throw a treat but
my hands are really empty
and he just looks at me like
"What. The. Fuck."

I want to stop
pretending

I want to stop
lying to me

I want to stop
thinking about drinking

I walked around
for a while

with a yellow rubber band
around my wrist
I snapped it
every time I thought
*A mimosa would be great
right about now*
but it just left me
angry and red
looking for whiskey

I want to stop
breaking
I want to bend instead
Like I should've bent over backwards
to make me your home
Like I should have bent at the knees
when you walked into a room
Like I should've never bent the truth
when it came to my feelings
about you
I should've told you
"you put stutters in my heart"
"you make me forget to exhale, inhale"
but then again "you make it
easier to breathe"

I want to stop
hiding all the time, too

3

it gets lonely like that
and I want to stop
missing you

I want to stop
remembering
the times you tucked me in at night
"Hospital corners"
you used to tell me
and you kissed me so softly and said
"Sweet dreams"
as if my dreams could be anything but
cotton candy with you

I want to stop
remembering
I want to stop
remembering that
needles bruising your skin
made you feel better than I ever did
I know
it doesn't work like that, darling
but I'm just telling you how I'm feeling
and it feels
like you
doped me right outta your memory

"I want to stop
believing"
"I want to stop
believing"

I don't care what Journey says
I want to stop
believing
you'll yo-yo back to me
and we would have this
movie-screen
drug-free
Happily-Ever-After ending
side by side or,
hand in hand or,
step by step,
you
aren't
coming
back
not
ever

I want to stop
thinking about forever
because now
when I consider forever
it blows my mind
you're not in it

I want to stop
all this starting over
I want to stop
living for a tomorrow
that will just never sober up

I want to stop
hoping for the same thing
every night
before I sleep
I want to stop
the "You and Me"

So.

I want to stop
cooking enough
food to feed a small army
after all
it's just me

I want to stop
walking down my street with
Resting Murderer Face

I want to smile
at everyone I meet

and I want the best
only the very best
for you

BRAT

I knew from the moment
I laid eyes on you
we were going to have filthy animal sex
the kind of sex you don't tell your closest friend about
because even they would be like
wow, what the fuck is wrong with you?

you want so very badly
to be able to scare me but
you don't
not your painted nails down my spine
not your hand around my throat
where you never squeeze quite hard enough

you don't say much
and I like it
it makes every threat you whisper
in my ear even sweeter
sweet like the kind of sting against my ass
sweet like your sweet tooth
scraping against my ribcage

listen
I'd walk on broken glass
to hear you call me your brat
because at least I'd be yours.

GO TO BED

She wakes with
thunderclaps at her back
the night before
she'd swallowed lightning bolts
which explains
the early morning jolt
even as a child
resting and awakening
never came easy
her mother laid her
on her back
when she was a baby
swaddled tightly
found her minutes later
spitting up salty seawater
and seaweed

Sleep doesn't come easy to me
these nights
not after her
I dream of her end
in a thousand different ways
I dream of fentanyl
I dream of blood
spreading like a blooming
across the concrete underneath
a 40-story building of
a tech company
that she would've never worked for

I think of two fistfuls of prescription pills
years of prescriptions
exploding in her perfect mouth
for once
not so tight-lipped
for once
not so lock-jawed
for once
open like the mouth of a tornado
when she slept next to me
that was the most restful sleep
she said
No sand under my tongue
no magician pulling
scarves from behind my esophagus,
no excessive bass thumps in my ears
she said

I say
it's because
I held on to her like children hold their breath
going through a tunnel
I trailed over her ribcage like
rubbing the cracks in a sand dollar
I say

She'd never felt so full
she had never felt so solid
she'd never been a real girl

until then, right then
no mermaid, stranded at sea
no swift and terrible alchemy
keeping her eyes peeled
stealing her sleeping
it was me
just me.

SMALL DEATH

She walks like Tina Turner
And she talks like a philosopher
And I wanted her
All of her
The moment I watched her mouth design my name.
My name had never sounded so Christmas Eve
Than right then
In August

In that average black t-shirt
And habitual cigarette
She looked so arctic
It was the hottest

Her entire body is nonchalant
But she gets mad like a God
And she weeps like Christ

When she kisses me,
It's like running from the bulls
In Pamplona
In the middle of a dive bar
In San Francisco

She's like a bruise
You can't stop poking at
I can't stop touching her
Even though she's all
Hot stoves

And cyclones

We fight like World War One
Screaming like car alarms
Throwing punches like boxers
We always do
There's never a break like
How there's no break
From laundry
Or bills to pay
I wouldn't change it for
A week of nothing but Fridays
She amazes me

And me?
I fuck with the lights on
I'm so terrified of things I can't see
I do everything so carefully

I tucked my moth-ridden heart
Into yards of bubble wrap
Mustering up the bravado
To ask her
To let me make her coffee
Every morning
I'd do it perfectly

When she left me
It was like lightning
Destroying a perfect sky
Like no clean water in a flood

Like falling on gravel
Skinning your palms
Like choking on
Your own tongue

She says
When it hits you
After you've pulled the
Needle from your vein
It feels like clear traffic
On the freeway
Like a hug from your mother
Like towels from the dryer
Like marshmallows over a fire

You just die
This small death
And then it's over

I miss watching her smile
Lazy
Like a cat
In the sunlight
I miss strolling my fingers
Up the bumps of her spine

She plays me like a piano
She throws me as far
As the eye can see
She loves as hard as a forty-hour workweek
She just doesn't love me

And it's like that
Sometimes
It's like that.

STERNUM

I collect bones
instead of tea sets
instead of coins that reek of blood
I collect bones

small ones
things that I find in the gutters
of paved all-American streets

squirrels and birds
sometimes a stray cat
they are tossed aside
but I whisper life into
their most vital instruments

the metacarpals
I attach to pale pink lace doilies
the pubis I frame with
the shiniest mahogany wood

when the sun is setting
the warmth of these parts
is stunning they capture all
the sun is leaving behind

when I met you
I met your bones too
embraced the phalanges with my own
hesitating for a moment before letting go

because I didn't want to let you go
even then

your skull is the most perfect
it's one of those I would string
glittered ropes of lavender through the eye sockets
your wrists are tiny, like the sound of a bell

your clavicle would split open
to release bright white moon light
I hope it never shatters to reveal it

when you left me
I didn't have a single bone to remember you by
not one femur
I was constantly ringing the doorbell of an empty estate
trying to breathe deeply in a body of water
scraping my nails against a brick wall

when you left me
I gave up my collection of bones
what's a sternum without its heart?

LOVER

I've titled this poem with your name
Scratched it into the wet concrete
Muck underneath my peeling fingernails
I wanted you to see
The solidity you cause
And the destruction of a perfectly blank slate
I don't know what to do with you
You know as well as I do
How a face can morph in the mirror
How a pillowcase full of bricks
Can feel like the still body of a lover
What ever should come of this
We are weaved
Fingers plaited into one another's
You drop me to my knees
Heart and ears ringing
Pleading for one more night
A single day
I know you barely have enough to give away
I've seen your pockets turned inside out
But the more I see of you
The more I want to give to you
Take everything
My gilded handcuffs
From when I had to trick them into staying
I am entirely lost
That is not a flaw
Lover
I am chewing the inside of my cheeks

Swallowing blood
Wondering if you can taste it on my mouth

BOI

Boi
you ain't shit
The words you say
give me brain freeze
Your fingertips
land like bullets
I have dreams
that you kill me
When I wake up
Blood's on my tongue
and my skin weeps
You ruin me
for every other boi to come after you
Calling me
sweetheartbabylove
before immediately
setting me on fire
You know you do
From the perspective of anyone

we're doomed

I know only three things

In my dreams
you kiss me while you drive
a letter opener between my ribs
Like I said before
you bring the sun to its knees

And you do the same to me

God.
But you ain't shit.

COME WITH ME

Rest your persistent bones
in a damp graveyard
with me
until they can't decipher
who is the dead
and who is the living.

THINGS I SHOULD'VE TOLD YOU

You were always too good for me
You were
You looked like a God
and you were a nightmare
You destroyed me
when you left and when you stayed
The second-hand smoke would've killed me eventually
Literally
You never cared about that
You must've cared about me
somewhere
sometime
kissing like fireworks
I should've said "I love you"
You would've told me *slow down, honey*
I would've said it again
S L O W L Y

REMOVE THE BONES

I hate the deflated
Inflatable lawn ornaments
Laid bare and forgotten
On the manicured lawns
The day after Christmas
I am that Santa often

Loud and glaring sounds
Often jointed
With our favorite holidays
Noises that remove the bones
From your skin
Leaving your insides raw
And hot to the touch
Leaving your outsides creaking
And freezing

I am persuaded to stay inside
In my heated home
With my dogs
Holding their skin and bones
Together
Pressed like a PB&J sandwich

I've grown weary of rituals
That I'm expected to love
The colors, the loud loud loud
The disappointing images
And disappointing people

The textures, the baubles
The envious gazes, the fogs
And hazes

I am just tired.

She left on a Tuesday

No packed lunches,
No missing shoes,
No suitcases full that were once empty
She Harry Houdini-ed straight out of me

I'm without mercy
And maybe I never had any
When I think of her
I think of her scowls,
Her tongue tripping
Right over "I-love-you"s
Skinning her knees raw on her begging
Her bloody aggression
Smelling of a meat factory, rotting

And.
She is in me relentlessly
She does not give in
Or loosen her grip
Like a fourth grader who believes
They can orbit the swingset if

They just swing hard enough
Like the alcoholic that believes
This will be the last one

Occupying space and time
Is the most painful feature
Of her utter disintegration
I write eulogy after eulogy
Comparing her love to the
Necessity of air
Her hair to the finest ropes of lavender
But I keep them hidden from everyone
How can you eulogize someone
Who is not gone gone
Just gone from me,

That Tuesday I went to every
Church service that I could find
I saw a tortured Jesus staring at me
From a stained glass window
The reds, yellows, blues
All taking on the burden of the sun
Nearly made me weep

But it would be a full year before
I would cry at all

I scrunched up my face
I pinched my skin
So hard I left bruises
In the shape of her home state
All over my body
I thought of the saddest things
In the world
I thought of us
My eyes were dusty

I wish those lawn ornaments
Could stay up all year long
Their ability and willingness
To be so full
I don't understand it but
God
Maybe I can.

BAPTIZE

I dreamt last night
that you were an escape artist
I'd come to watch you elude
Squinting against piercing lights
I never reach for my glasses
even when they're right there
I wanted you to be a quick blur

Your mother was a tightrope walker
Your father, an extremist
Your sisters, all acrobats

When you were three
your parents padlocked
your compact body in the bathtub
held your dark head under bubblegum-scented waters and waited
When you emerged free of chains
they gave you one red M&M

You never see me
I was there for the Escapism Challenge
It had taken the man from Birmingham five years
to make those handcuffs.
56 minutes later and I counted every one
You were paraded around on the shoulders of The World's Largest Man
looking smug and uncomfortable
when you were delicately set on your feet
I watched the Bearded Lady smack a kiss on your lips
My skin grew too tight for all of the memories inside of it

I never believed in you
never took you as gospel
the way some people do

When you escaped me
It was the biggest feat of your career

DRAIN THE ENTIRE SEA

Lasso the moon
Drag her kicking and
screaming
from the center of the
sky
Tell the stars to
say their goodbyes

Set roots on fire
Watch the flame
climb skyward
dance in the ashes

Muzzle songbirds
Clasp your hands around
the throats of hummingbirds

Shave a lamb bald
and lay naked in its wool
Slide the knife between
it's 3rd and 4th rib
because you've always
"wanted a red sweater"

And then there's the
matter of me

Would you
gather yourself

down on bended knee
in front of a crowded subway
platform
and tell me you're leaving me

Would you take that
same knife
time and a lack of regret
rusting it
run the blade slowly
round my neck
a few times
so I'd feel comfortable in the fear

Would you ever
Would you ever just stay
Bet it

Bet it all.

FOUNDATIONS

I didn't want to touch her first
I couldn't stand how lovely
Her mouth was so
I didn't stand at all
My body was searing
My toes crystallized
Couldn't explain it if I wanted to

I didn't want to kiss her first
I walked over flaming coals
Soles extinguishing them and
Pressing them into diamonds
I placed handfuls
Into her impatient palms
She didn't say a word
She didn't have to

I didn't want to run to her bed
But I did
My options were lacking
My need elephantine

I strapped my chilly feet into
The palest pink pointe shoes
Fingers brushing their icy exterior
Ignoring my frostbitten fingers
I ran to her

It was easy to tune out

The *creakingcrackingcroaking*
Coming from my shoes
Easy to speed through agony
When I lose my heart
I lose it totally
When I am somebody's
They have all of me

My glaciers-for-feet shattered

I didn't want to love her first

ATTENDING AN AA MEETING
WITH YOUR EX-GIRLFRIEND

We held hands
Not just during the prayer
We held hands the entire time
I had 96 days clean
She had a few hours
I hate that word
"Clean"
What did it make the people who were still using?
What did that make me 97 days ago?
Shotgunning wine and earnestly wondering if anyone had coke
Dirty girl
I wanted to ask why her skin felt so cold
I considered wrapping my body around her
Arms interlaced through her ribs
Mouth pressed against her forehead I whispered instead
Mouth to her ear
"You are okay"
She smiled then
Shaky and watery
For the first time since our stiff, formal embrace at the church doors
Her eyes remained obediently on the speaker
Her hand was hard
The skin
I was with her for months and
I never noticed those callouses
Just like I never noticed how she bounced her leg when she was nervous
I never noticed a lot of things
When we stand for the prayer

Grasping a stranger's hand
With my free one
I'm struck by how tall she is
But she's hunched over
Attempting to crawl inside herself
She's terrified and when I'm honest with myself
I am too
God, grant me the serenity to accept the things I cannot change
Our relationship is held together with bubblegum and shoelace string
Courage to change the things I can
We're a shitty science project, volcanoes exploding off cue
And wisdom to know the difference
There's no one I'd rather clean up with than you.

HYMNS FOR A TUESDAY AFTERNOON

Using her pointed
witch nails
to scratch
geometric patterns on my
stark naked hip bones
using her tongue
to soothe away
the sharp

Mercy.

Gazing
starry-eyed and
lazy-mouthed
staring down at her
beaming black head
diligently working
between my parted thighs
I would part
every single part of me
for her
if I could

Mercy.

Holding her in my fluttering
palms like a prayer
calling/ responding
gospel hymns
in perfect harmony

with her groans

Mercy.

Setting off
smoke alarms
busily kissing in the kitchen
she passes her
excitement to me
through our mouths
like blowing smoke
back and forth
until there's nothing
left

Mercy.

There is
nothing left
everything we've
tried to recycle
is just trash

Everyone sees that
and I know we're past that
exalted stage but
for God's sake
pick up the phone
and show me a little

Mercy.

THE FOG

I dated a girl from Inverness, California. It's where they shot that movie *The Fog*. She took me to her childhood home. We fucked on her childhood bed. I started my period, staining her childhood robot sheets. She said, "It was alright, honey." She was just happy to see me.

We talked late into the night, early into the morning. Just the stars listening. Their eyes didn't tell our secrets. Not even a sly glance, not even a furtive wink.

She told me about her childhood. How she remembered mostly screams. All of the horror screens brought to you by the monsters sleeping sweetly a floor below us. Bruises etched into thin skin so frequently they might as well have been tattoos. Baby teeth knocked loose by adult fists. Trespassing the "Stay Out" sign posted on her childhood bedroom door.

I don't ask why she shakes like she's drenched when I run my hand down her spine, why she's terrified of the dark and yelling. Can you imagine a 30 year old woman wetting the bed because I accidently grabbed her wrist in a certain way that reminded her of a certain day when she was small?

And shattered a drinking glass; it exploded, fragments blooming across the carpet. Dad exploded too, dragging her by her teeny wrist, tiny like the sound of a bell.

I learn to touch her like I'm disarming a bomb, parts of her are landmines and she looks at me with wide eyes.

When we go downstairs for breakfast, I sit at her childhood dining table, stare at her father's eyes. I want to launch a thousand shards into his beer gut. I want to wrap a bear trap around his throat. Slow like the syrup on our pancakes, I push my drinking glass from the childhood table. It explodes.

We drive off into the fog.

WINDED

May I speak complete
sentences around you
May I breathe on my own
in full
not these brief
gasps for you

I am never so frail
or humble
I have never stammered
or fumbled

I am dusty lungs
and ocean eyes
I am following
your mountain trail
without a map

I am always somehow
lost
even with the
navigation systems on
always scanning for landmarks
searching for things I recognize
that are no longer there

Now I pinpoint your arms as home.

COCOON

Do you believe in magic?
Is that a weird question for a first date?
But do you?
Did you have to think twice?

I believe in a million silly things
That aren't actually silly.
They're just facts.

Like

I believe that when newborns
See that fluorescent light
They think they're about to die from
The Bright.

I believe that butterflies have feelings.
I believe the evolution of a butterfly
Is painful.

I believe the book
The Very Hungry Caterpillar
is about America's consumerist greed.

I believe the sky has feelings too.
That's why it pours.
It poured the day she left.
I did too.
It snowed the next week.

I believe it can snow in the sweltering
heat
On the hottest day
In New York City.
My ice nearly dissolved on the day she
Took my face in her hands
And spoke only my name.

I believe you can match your heartbeats
to a lover's.
When her heart stops before a kiss
You can stop yours too.
When her heart
sloooooooows
To match
The swagger of your gait
Yours should waltz, too.

I believe the women who bend over soil
Planting seeds are magic.
Hands covered in soaked Earth
Fingers plucking the strings
To feed and quake the
World.

I used to believe she was magic
The way she could disappear/reappear.

I believe keeping rabbits in hats

Is cruel.
I want to free all the rabbits
In the magician's hat,
Patiently waiting to be liberated
But
I don't know how to abracadabra yet.

I believe there's no such thing as a Bad
Person.
Just regular people who
Weren't held enough or
Regular people who
Weren't kissed on their open mouths or
Regular people who said goodbye too
soon and
Regular people who got left too.

I believe palm lines tell the future.
I got mine read after she left
And had to dodge questions about why
My lifeline was sliced so short
cut off at the peak.

Would you believe it if I told you

I still have those dreams
Where she's in a drowning car
Holding onto her precious breath
Water creeping up her jaw, nose, neck?
I am the only one that can save her.
I am the only one.

I'm on the shore,
Watching blank-faced
And I wave good-bye to her.
It's that ice in me again.

Can you believe it?

But do you believe in magic?
What would you change?
Would you tell your mom you love her?
Would you go to prom with
The girl you secretly adored?
Would you save her life?
Would you take her back?

SEA CUCUMBERS

I dreamt last night that you were a walrus
and I had a lucrative walrus-hunting business.
I wanted your tusks to make into fine jewelry
for rich wives.

I stalked you for days
eventually becoming charmed by your
comedic ways.
Clumsily diving, giving high-fives
barking your approval of the fish we threw
into the ocean.

When I stabbed you on the fourth day
red mist blanketing my face
clouds weighing down my timid shoulders
It was the most difficult thing I'd ever done.
I kept a tusk for my own
but pieces of you don't make a you
I'm not sure what that means, love.

But I've been looking up the dream
interpretation of walruses for eight hours.
Does it mean she's alive or dead?
Alive or dead?

Your name sits in my stomach like lead.
I've swallowed it again.
Every time I said your name
I counted.

I knew I wouldn't have the privilege of saying
it for very long.
You're not the type to let me have you
for very long.

The first time we fought, I traced my fingertip
over your mouth and you forgave me for
crimes I was framed for.
Just like that
you took me back.

Now I'm sleeping all day
drinking myself earnest again
dreaming it could be like that
kissing in the opera seats
fucking with the windows open
wishing for the same thing
every night, before we dream

I'm just here
Wondering what walruses eat.

WHY NOW?

I remember you blushing
up at me from bent knees

I remember crouching on the
church steps
swaying to the choir

I remember twisting off
bottle caps
with our sparkly teeth

I remember you fingering
my hair
asking for a kiss
slurry-voiceboxed and starry-eyes

I remember burying
sweet-nothings
into wet concrete

I remember wearing nothing
but yards of stars
like gilded capes

I remember sitting on the bus
entwined in one another

I remember sitting on the bus
in opposite seats.

DIALECTICS

This is hard to write
 and
I'm writing it.
I dreamt you came to me whole.
I was your target range.

You are everything.
and
You are nothing.

I imagined you used up.
Character wrung out of you.
This is called self-deception.
This is called preaching the truth.

The last time I saw you
my lungs were viced.
My kneecaps were a porcelain doll's.

You were a bully with a slingshot.
and
You wore a red cape.

I don't make sense to you.
and
I'm speaking plain English to you.

Stark and white as hospital bed sheets.
Why can't you understand me?
You never got me.
and
We spoke volumes with our palms.

We finished each other's sentences.
Those lengthy, raspy screams.

We complement.
We're separate.

Last night, late
I scribbled your name on a napkin.
Shoved it inside a blue balloon.
I spoke into it all my sorrys and I love
yous.
I pressed it to my chest
then
handed it to the moon.

I am over you.
and
Forever suffocating under you.

SUNRISE GHAZAL

Magnetic with the sun
We are burning
Thrashing limbs and ashy breath, forever

Being cool is an exercise in futility
It hasn't served us well in, forever

I've never known warmth but in your arms like that I found myself
praying for, forever

When it finally burns out, we find ourselves
Looking where it was, forever

COGNITIVE

I dreamt last night
you were my therapist
Your office was blue
Made me feel like I was back-stroking
instead of walking
The only cushioned thing was your couch
You made me lie on it and
tell you about my ex

You wanted to know how I felt in my body when *"she"*
looked at me
it made my heart sprint
I told you
My skin felt too tight
My eyes gathered tears in grocery bags
You called it an intense love
I don't disagree

In our next session you have me
draw an outline of my body
with a wide black marker on a large sheet of paper
The smell reminded me of grade school
erasers and holding sticky hands in a line
two by two
I draw the outline of a four-legged monster

You have me lie down on a fresh sheet
and you trace my body

Inside of me, everything is marathon-running
Ants travel up and down my inner thigh
I breathe in half beats
You drew me small and tenuous
And you've added wings

In our last session
you asked me
to make a list
of everything that scared me
I told you
"We're going to be here for the rest of our lives"
At the top of my list were your fingertips

LIFE AFTER

I am waiting
for you to say it back

I am not being coy
I am not playing games

It's just that you
put earthquakes in my fingertips
Making it difficult to write
the things I want to say

Things like,

I want to take you idly
unhurriedly
as if
there are eyes on my hands
and I want to see every inch of you

The night I met you
I imagined you wrecking me
I would call you *sweetheart* as you
played your oxfords
over my softened heart
until there would be nothing but
flattened debris

And I'd dust it all off

and say,
"You can do it again
do it for the rest of my life"

If there's one thing that I know
about lust
it doesn't last forever
Its shelf life is brief and quickly
completely forgotten
It is severed into pieces
Each fragment
scattered in various places in the
backyard
and buried in the Earth

When the dog digs it up years later
you will tell your new love

Look how silly I was
Never knew love, really
Waited my whole life for you, really
Every second was a wasted second,
really

Really.

I can always feel the moment they start
to slip away

My grasp on their
strands of hair get even looser
I stop all my New Bride quivering
And they notice and they take note
 and they're upset

And then we are gone

But you

I've thanked the moon for you
I've sat under her pregnant belly
Blew blue, congratulatory balloons and
sent them her way

Now we speak nightly
She blesses my forehead
Sanctified
with exalted ocean water

She blows cool winds across my
sometimes
grief-stained cheeks
She tells me about you

Tells me how the first time you saw her
The Moon
You were terrified at your own lack of
comprehension

Tells me how you used to kneel at her
alter
Before you found salvation kneeling
between women's legs

When you are gone
I will be done with the moon
I will be done with stars and sunlight a
soil
I will cut my floor-length hair
the hair I've grown since knowing you
I'll place the refuse in a silver locket
braided and cut with lace
mourning jewels

I will ask you to wear it around your
noble neck
And you will refuse

Lay my stark white bones
at the tabernacle of faith
Divinity
Honesty
Prose and poetry

Lay my fractured bones at your
careless feet

GRATITUDE

You are changing me
From the innards out
You've corrupted my chest
Into always breaking
You've atrophied my leg muscles
So I'm only staying
I am not complaining

You are a snow-capped cabin
With a fireplace inside
You are terrifying
And Holy
You are every waking night terror
Underneath my four-post bed

I'm not used to carving lust poems
Into my inner arms
I'm not used to sitting on
The ledge of tears
All the time

You could devour my heart
Pierce your canines
Into my right atrium
Ruby juices trickling
Down your chin
And I would say,
"Thank you."

ALTERNATIVES TO SPLITTING
YOUR SKIN WITH MY TEETH

Shoot each other in the chest while wearing bulletproof vests.

Pull out your tooth.

Tie one end of a string to a doorknob
the other to your front tooth and
slam the door.
Slamming doors.
You're always slamming doors
in my direction.

Read from the same worn, leather-brown bible

Because the only thing, you said, that can save us now, is if Christ himself
descended from heaven
and made us say our sorries
and forced us to hug.

I could braid your hair too tight

Like so tight
Like so tight
I can squeeze dialogue out of the brown ropes.

We could write love poems

one line each.
but I worry my lines will compare you to a stained glass angel
and yours would compare me to an atom bomb in a china shop.

We could touch each other slowly.

I'd have to prepare my cast-iron suit.
Your hands have been sandpaper these days.

I could melt peppermints all delicate on your inner thigh.

I could drain the moon of its milk to give it to you as a birthday present

that the other women could never give to you.
not her or her or that one or the other one.

Leave hickeys on the pads of your fingers.

Shove tiny nail scissor blades under each other's fingernails

Suck the blood.

Spit out the blood

Examine the blood as if it is a Rorschach test

I see butterflies.
You see corpses.

I wrote a poem a little while ago
called "How to Eat Your Lover."
We've moved past cannibalism to straight incineration.
We are setting each other on fire every night.
It isn't the heat we were used to

Smoking bed sheets, the warmth rocking us to sleep.
This strips your skin in layers
Burns so hot, you're too stunned to remember how to scream.

Pour the gasoline.

We could pour the gasoline.

.

BLUEBIRD

I am walking downstairs on my tippy toes
I am floating, sleeping over my bed
I am cartwheeling towards committing
I am backbending towards home

She is my ending
I consider The After Her
And I see nothing
No colors
No other women with pale
velvet skin
No other women who dream
Only in simile for me

I feel the emptiness on my palms
It is shattered windows
It's pinecones
It's crumpled binder paper
Balled in my fist
Giving me microscopic cuts
so small
I didn't even know they existed

Until
I am using my hand to wipe the saltwater
off my face
And the burning is of such
a magnitude
it almost feels sweet

I know
I test the limits of her sanity
I know
She walks on bird bones around me
My edges are frayed
My softness is used up
Her patience has dried up
and I am the largest imaginable boat
And she stays

We create fireworks displays
We love like war isn't an option
Like Forever is actually For Ever
Like the rest of time and then beyond it
We love like sailors coming home from the seas
Smelling of weeds and terrifying loneliness
We love hard and bloody like a steel worker's fingertips
We love with fragility, finally

I spent the majority of my twenties
Wishing on every fog-misted streetlight
For someone to be so shatterable with
This is her
The ending

QUERY

I imagine the inside of your mouth
tastes clear like water
I imagine your head in my hands
is weightless

I imagine your ribcage will link with my own
I imagine your heartbeat
will follow mine too
I imagine mine will race
with yours a close second

I imagine we will burn in a terrible way
I imagine you will groan when
I take your index finger into my mouth
I imagine I will carry its salt
under my tongue for the rest of my life

I imagine the skin at your neck
will not give easy
when I dig my canines in,
it just will not split
I imagine you will swallow me whole.

CRUSH

You probably already know this
but lately,
when I see your smile
my heart feels like explosions
beats like
I've just run a four-minute mile, now
isn't that something?

I can finally feel my own red heart
beating in my terrified chest
And you're the reason why
Why I jump out of bed at 6 in the
morning and obsessively check my
texts
and
You're the reason why I
feel like I'm being set on fire
most of the time
why I'm smiling like I'm five and
it's school picture day and
I've got my favorite bow in my hair

How come before I see you
I can't find anything right to wear

It's like
nothing is good enough
and everything is just wrong

Would you mind it if I came to you
naked?
Wearing nothing but this
big grin
And I held your face in my hands
so that I could finally see you
See that you're always
going to be scared of loss
and that
sometimes you really miss your mom
see that when you're looking at me
you're wondering if
I'm gonna rip you apart
like everyone else
I've never been like everyone else
I'm not gonna start now

Darling,
on our first date
you shook like a leaf
And me?
Well, I just couldn't believe
you were looking at me
like that, like
I hung the moon to make you laugh
And you
you with those
constellations in your eyes
and earthquakes in your hands

I thought

She's going to cut me down at the spine
She's going to bend me at the knees
She's going to make me wish these
Butterflies were wishes
I'd wish for you to be mine

A million different times

Because what I am is absolutely yours
Everyday I'm waiting
until I can hear you call my name
And, okay
I know you're poly
But I think my name
should be the only name you ever say
Because nobody says it like you
Nobody does anything quite like you

I want to know where you come from
I want to know who gave you
those dimples
I want to know who you smile like
and where you learned to laugh
like that
with your whole body
filling the whole room

I want to know why you never curse
and who taught you those

Good Midwestern Manners
Take me to your hometown
Show me where your father
showed you to ride a bike
And where you kissed a boy and realized
you didn't like it
Take me to where I can kiss you
under stars we can actually see
I want to shake your mama's hand
while you tell her
we're just really close friends

Lover
I want to sleep in your childhood bed
I want to lie staring at the same walls
you spent so many nights staring at
I wish I knew you then
So I could tell you
you'd turn out just fine
That you'd never lack for young
moonstruck girls
who'll write you love poems
tuck them into your pockets
before you go

I want to hear how you feel about me
I don't want any of that bullshit about
too much, too soon
to come between me and you
I want to know what
goes on in your body

when you see me running to you
tripping on my own two feet
giddy with the possibility that
you may want me as much as I want you
Woman
you are so fucking handsome
And my favorite thing
about the way you look
is that it's the
least interesting thing about you

Tell me everything
I want to swing from your tongue
Touch me everywhere
Play my body like a well-loved
instrument

You probably already know this
But there's nothing like hearing it
again and again
You are everything I've ever wanted

NAMING THE STARS

I read once
that the harder you try
to remember
a dream
the further away
from you it runs

Is it the same
for nightmares?

In my dreams
she is kept Holy
there is no
cursing my name
there is no
hand slithered around my neck
there is no
black eye under layers of concealer
no
thinly concealed threats in my ear

There is only her
and those eyes
like fluorescent bulbs
there is only
magnetic hands
and ribcages
there is only
Naming the Stars

after our future children
that one night
on her rooftop
flat on our backs
limbs knotted
wearing nothing
but the night sky

And when I dream that up
and I pick up that telephone
to call
I nightmare the time
she smashed my head against
the wall so hard
I saw the stars
we'd named Amelia
Michael
and Abigail

Queer women get
left out of the
domestic violence conversation
so often
I thought my bruises
were of my own creation

Thought I'd
painted on the
midnight blacks and

blues as blue as
her eyes
while she slept silent
beside me
not at all the
Tick.

Tick.

Tick.

Bomb.

You knew she was.

But my body has never fibbed
my ribs still
creaked from the fractured cracks
my vision still
blurred from praying at
the glaring moon

Still.

I ate nothing but ashes
the day she left
wept mourning songs
walked on hot coals

We existed in circles

Passing through
Iloveyous
screamed so many times
I wondered if she'd
run out of breath
the way I did
with her hands
wrapped around
my neck

So   many
gentle caresses
it seemed impossible
her hand would ever
turn claw again

Andthenandthenandthen

She says
I was flirting
with the girl at the grocery store

Or.

I wore
a bitchy tone
that looked awful on me

Or.

My smile when she walked

in the front door
wasn't traffic light bright enough

And the wheel would spin again
and the cycle would begin
and I'd end up on the hardwood floor
again.

Is it true
what they say about
dreams?

Will my grip on
her already translucent strands of hair
loosen
a bit everyday?

And what of this nightmare?

I wouldn't mind this exorcism,
the forgetting,
the loosening.

My fear has boiled over
sizzling when the refugees
hit the stovetop,
smelling of charred milk and her

Every day there's a little less
Every day I am a little more.

EXPIRING

Would you go to my funeral
Old Love?
Would you throw down handfuls
of earth and sunflower petals
on my casket?
Did you know they were my favorite?

You didn't.

Did you know my favorite place on myself
is the space between my fingers?

You didn't.

Did you know it was the only place I liked
some days?

Did you know this icicle of a globe
these glacier hearts ruined me?

Did you know I grew brave until I didn't?

Did you know that when I fell in love
with the tips of your hair
you were drunk?
Bent over a toilet

And when I fell out of love with them
you were running your hands through them

hand signaling,
signing that you were done with me

Did you know I could hold on to a single memory for the rest of my life?

Ancient Love
All we were
screams and backing away from one another
A let-down
Guards up.

Gray Love,
Would you come to my funeral?
Would you cry buckets of blue?
Would your cheeks turn red with anger?
Is your grief black?
Would you show me your colors?

Let people see your sorrow
Weep
Wail
Say you'll miss me
And never mean it.

Wasted Love
Would you sit in the front row?
Reserved for those closest to me
Would you shoulder your way in?
Sit your falseness right next to my New Love
Would she show her sharp teeth?
Would she too be deceived by your show?

So.
Would you come to my funeral?
Throw your body into the grave
Press your body to the casket?
Stay until they pull your body away
Would you stay?

CLASSROOM GUIDE

VULNERABILITY

In relationships, sometimes it feels easier to hide our true emotions because it feels disagreements are draining or unnecessary. What are some ways we can be honest and open for our loves and ourselves?

PROMPTS

Create a mental check list. Has there ever been a time where our decisions are actually stabbing us in the back instead of keeping us protected? Try to recall these moments, looking in to the outside. Write a poem that exams hurt and loneliness and the way we are pushed down. Try to try write a list poem to uncover the alternatives.

REPRESENTATIVE POEMS:

"Alternatives to Splitting Your Skin With My Teeth," "Expiring," "Reverse Midas Touch"

ACKNOWLEDGEMENTS

There are so many wonderful, kind people in my life that it would be impossible to name them all but here are some:

I appreciate the folks at Nomadic Press for giving me the opportunity to publish my little love poems. Thank you for the patience, kindness, and inspiration.

I'm very thankful for my chosen family: Madison, James, and MacKenzie for putting up with my midnight, panicked pleas to edit poems and so many more things.

I am madly appreciative for my partner, Grant Kien, always motivating me to do better and being an overall good human. Love you.

I love my family. Thank you to my aunties for the swag I spent years trying to replicate. Thank you to my baby cousins. I will always protect and support you. And you will always be babies to me. To my mother and Nana. I'll always try to be good and make you proud.

I want to give Nomadic Press editor, Nina Sacco, major props. Thank you so much for working closely with me on this book. You're amazing and so supportive. I appreciate you.

I'm so grateful to all the literary folks for letting me perform at your shows, publishing my works and being among the most talented people I've ever met.

Finally, thank you to all the lovers that I write about. I think of you often and fondly and I will forever.

Thank you.

ANNA ALLEN

Born in Stockton, California, Anna Allen comes from a world filled with playground adventures and forever pinky promises. She has only recently entered the published literary scene, performing at slams, open mics, and featured shows. So far, Anna has found so much inspiration in her fellow poets and is always trying to reach the same level of honesty and vulnerability. You can find more of her work at littledeathlit, The Scriblerus, and TRACK//FOUR. Keep up with Anna at *annaallenwrites.wixsite.com/website.*

OTHER WAYS TO SUPPORT
NOMADIC PRESS' WRITERS

In 2020, two funds geared specifically toward supporting our writers were created: the **Nomadic Press Black Writers Fund** and the **Nomadic Press Emergency Fund**.

The former is a forever fund that puts money directly into the pockets of our Black writers. The latter provides up to $200 dignity-centered emergency grants to any of our writers in need.

Please consider supporting these funds. You can also more generally support Nomadic Press by donating to our general fund via nomadicpress. org/donate and by continuing to buy our books. As always, thank you for your support!

Scan here for more information and/or to donate.
You can also donate at nomadicpress.org/store.